AF583282

A Delightful Harmony of Spirit

A Delightful Harmony of Spirit

AN AGREEMENT WITH THE SOUL

NUSRAT JABEEN

Notion Press

Old No. 38, New No. 6
McNichols Road, Chetpet
Chennai - 600 031

First Published by Notion Press 2016

ISBN 978-1-946390-57-8

Dedication

I dedicate this book to my parents, *for* their endless support and without them; my *feelings* were imperfect while writing.

PREFACE

'A delightful harmony of spirit' (an agreement with the soul) mainly relate to an account of expressing and distinctive thoughts of 'charismatic beauty' of soul languages. So, a notion reflects to the body's soul with wonderful agreement, where all the amusing strengths and will-power give a warm touch to the soul. So, delightful harmony is a big connection to the strength of mind that gives a high degree of satisfaction. Though, when we indulge in it; then we meet of great pleasure and come from the God's eyes.

As an author, this book is an inspiration for readers who have isolated life and never felt their soul voice. The notion behind this book is to set my views in a conscious and delicate way. Apart from that cuddle my individual quality of person who really depends on an originator of innovative ideas with pleasant mind. Furthermore, I had not any prior experienced to express my writing while I do have potential sources of inspiration who motivated me for good writing through the way of diverse thoughts.

The topic was chosen because of the heavenly connection of the heart I have for the spirit and how it effects have affected mind. I artistically expressed myself on my topic where I accept the sort of a poem; the poem is entitling 'A Great Satisfaction', and we human being has a spiritual agreement *from* the God, who grants great satisfaction *for* a *full* time agreement till the death *of* time.

Before I *finish*, the target audience *for* my portfolio are teenagers, adults, ageing people and all person *for* whom I propose to deliver my voice to the spectator's soul *of* mind.

ACKNOWLEDGEMENTS

I express my sincere thanks to all without whose help and support this work cannot be completed as it is now. Here, due to space constraint, it is very difficult to name them all, so I mentioned only few of them.

First of all, I begin with the name of the Almighty, which is most important; I thank the eternal, most blessed creator of the universe, for always having showered his blessings upon me.

I owe a debt of gratitude to my parents who stood always behind me like a wall and supported when I was disappointed and feeling low; and also encouraging me to complete the book. My parents are real source of inspiration for me who sacrifices their life happiness only for us and their life surrounds around us.

This work was completed with the inspiration, motivation, encouragement and guidance provided by my adored sister Dr. Shahla Tabassum. I express my heartful thanks to her for dedicating her time to read and discuss all my writings, providing professional guidance and support to shape my thoughts and provide invaluable input during the process. I learned a great deal from her wealth of experiences, passion for work and dedication to her responsibilities.

Last but very important I sincerely thanks to Mr. Naveen Valsakumar (Co-Founder) of publication house 'Notion Press' and team, who shaped my career goals through publication guidance and supporting me with all the professional helps I needed.

SOUL NATURE

Sign On Myself As A Human Being;
A Victim Of God's Creature,
Parcel Me A City Of Divine;
Who Gave Me This Impulsive Time,

To Meet 'A Soul Energy' On Earth;
Be Blessed 'To Stand' On Strength,
Then 'A Puzzling Spirit' Leaps Up My Life,
So, Please Pause My Nature...

Born And Brought Up With Formal Attitude;
Only Concern To My Expression,
'I Would Like To My Polite Nature;
Who 'Gave Me' This Creature',

Hey Look! Always End With The 'Admire Senses';
Where No Place To Tough Soul,
Remarkable Feelings 'Come Out' With Gripping;
To Touch Me 'An Instant' Healing,

Because Of A Guiltless Girl;
Flexible My Nature But Fit 'In To This' Open Creature,
'I Would Like My Polite Nature;
Who Gave Me This Creature',

Scarcely To Take Off My Veil Of Desire;
While 'Clinging To Trance' An Aesthetic Life,
Merely Simple Lives Create Their Own Story;
No More Desire; No Memory Story,

Human Nature 'Ties' On Common Goals;
Where It Patch To 'Challenge' And 'Charge',
'I Would Like My Polite Nature;
Who Gave Me This Creature',

Move Onto 'Positive Gesture' Of My Attire Nature;
Act Like 'Silent Feature' On This Creature,
Always 'Proactive' Like A Flame Of Fire;
Barely 'Dull' When I 'Feel Alone' To Take Hire,

A Radiant Life To 'Draw Me' Under The Shed Of Hope;
And Path 'Arrives' On Actual Way,
'I Would Like My Polite Nature;
Who Gave Me This Creature',

Notches 'All The' Negative Thoughts;
While 'Human' Plays On Flexible Downing Age,
In Hence, 'Human Nature' Reflects On Versatile Trait;
The Same 'An Art Of Life' We Create,

To 'Wrap' The Human Nature In Fold;
Only It Would 'Portray' On Unusual Proverb Say,
'I Would Like My Polite Nature;
Who Gave Me This Creature',

FRAGRANCE OF AN ANGEL

A 'Bonny Cutie Pie' Of Paradise Smiles;
Leave 'Behind The Mark' Brought Me 'A Place' Safely,

Dream About 'A Bunch Of Heavenly Haven';
Put Out 'As A Fable' Of God's World,
Nonetheless 'Kissed My Dream Tightly';
Also 'Walked Around' By Bare Foot,

A Little Finger 'Be Touch' My Hand;
Present 'A Warm Feeling' Ended The Shiver,
Marvelous 'Jannat-Ul-Firdaus' The Uppermost;
And 'Top Eternal Place' In Paradise To Lay Down,

Stretch To 'The Blessed Tree' Put On Palms;
Pomegranates; Dates; Olives; Figs; Grapes; Tooba And Sidrah...
'God Likened All' That's Why Shaped;
In The 'Earnest Heart' As Bears Fruits Of Good Deeds,

It's All 'Appear' Under The Light Of Heavens;
All God's 'Fresh Gifts Unite',
And Depend 'Nature's Staple Food' Of Man,
Also, Paradise People Clothes Ready;

'To Calyces' Be Fond Of 'Outer Sheath' Of It's Flowers,
Without Blinking My Stuck Eyes;
Istabraq: A Gold Decoration On Cloth...
A Fine Silk Worn Said Sondos,

Although, 'Harir And Harirah' A Word Of Silk;
'Floored The Paradise' With A 'Salsabeel Fountain' Blow Down,
We Knock To The Next Door;
The 'Entire Nutrients' Raise In A Proportional Ways,

'Eye Catching Angels' Have A Beautiful Garden Of Heaven;
Take To 'The Air' With 'Her Mesmerizing Wings',
I Felt 'Thirst' Then Had A Heavenly Flavour Of 'Zanjabee' Drinks;
Like A Bitter, Sweet And Warming Taste Of Ginger,

Let's Come Down...
To The End Of 'Lulu' And 'Luluah' Pearl;
A Glittery, Authentic And An Auspicious Gift Of God's,
So, Take Me Off...

Towards The Covering Shell Of Protection;
Which Gives Me Sooth Forever,
Asked Again 'To Him' Any 'Sins Turn To The Sinner' Then Replied;
Yeah! A Greater One And Smaller One,

A Flourish 'Baby Hand' Of My Gorgeous Sensation;
Make 'A Record Of Paradise' To The Best Believers,
'Loud Say' Came From The 'Cracked Body' Of Mine;
Awoke Suddenly! So 'Smile' With A Sense Of Mind,
'Although 'Fragrance Of An Angel' Scattered...
To 'The Whole Room' With Positive Vibes...'

SNOOZE MONSTER

A Long Time Ago In A Hey Day...
Slept With My Beloved Mom And I,
There Is No Fairy Tales Point;
Only Story A Fact Of Time,

A Factual Tale Creates...
In A 'Sense Of Mine' In An Ode Line,
An Ugly Terrifying Night;
Be Asleep By Way Of Mine,

Wondering Wonder...
Be Indulge My Sweet Dream,
Oh Heavenly Felt! Means No Other One 'Butt In';
No 'More Than Other' Only 'Motto' A Good Thing,

Be In A Hand...
'Embraced My Mother' To See A Nice Dream,
Sooner 'Got To Disturb' To See 'An Ugly' Wicked Person;
'Huge Thing Appears' Also...

Pressing Neck Of My Mother,
Leave! Leave! Go Away 'Screamed Loud' Be Mumble,
Oh! Unusual Being 'Just Fade Away' To My Vision,
And 'Screamed' Save! Save! Requested Shorn Of Him,

You! Massive Monster...
'I Will Slay You' If Not Run Off,
Furiously! Hit To Him 'From My Leg' With Energetically;
'As Understand' Than 'My Whole Body' Shook down,

My 'Adorable Mother'...
Slapped Me On My Both Cheek;
Also Told Me 'On Hold',
What Happened In Sleep? You Dupe Kid..,

No Issue Mother...
Only Saw 'A Giant Snooze Monster',
To 'Wipe Out' My Wet Face;
So, Slept Again With My Tears,

Up In The Morning Shine...
Told The Full Nightmare Story,
Ha..Ha..Ha! Laughing Zone High;
With Glory Gone Last Night,

VOYAGE IN THE SKY

When Decided To See The World...
While I Tired off To Work,
To Patch Up The Fading Work;
Have Packed My Luggage,

Abscond From The Native Land...
And Fetch Up The High Move,
Through Far Above The Ground;
My Heart Goes Down,

Brought The World Into My Buck...
And Spirit Goes Peak,
'Have Cheery' Frame Of Mind;
Enfold With Reserved Smile,

Recall A Hey Day...
Next To Way Of Fluctuating Mind,
Wrap The Wait To Tight My Travel;
And Take Off By Jet,

To Trek Into Sky...
I Really Enjoy To Each Countryside,
Be 'An Enter' In The Air;
Soul Floats In The Blue Sky,

Cuddling To Voyage In The Sky...
A Rainbow Comes From Outside,
What A Scenery? Gazed Outside.........!
Look At That! Look At That! A Shimmering
Sun Come Inside,

While Float Onto The Sky...
Feel Like As A Child,
Yeah, I Really Flourished;
From The God's Eye,

God's Art 'At Hand' To VIBGYOR...
Sense Of Seven Colors,
Violet, Indigo, Blue, Green, Yellow, Orange And Red,
All Colours Met 'To Get An Fresh Idea' Of God's,

Scratch The Cross State...
By Changing The Weather's Bye,
To Leak A Voyage In The Sky;

Naive Wish Drop On The Wit,
Close My Eyes 'To Lost My Sight' So 'Wondering' In The Skies,
Every Flash Stand 'To Say' Alive Alive And Alive..........!

MEDDLING SMASH BOOK

Preserved 'Lots Of Ally' Inside My Engaging Heart;
Hold A 'Piece Of Paper' To Frame In A Book Sheet,
Be A Record 'In Bang Book' Really Felt Fervent;
While Set In A Flashback Moment,

So, Let's Have Start...
To Recognize My Pal Friend Forever,
I'm Proudly Known As 'Slam Book' And Other Say;
Scrap Book, Bang Book, Smash Book And So On,

The Day 'This Earth' Was Blessed...
On When I 'Landed' In This Stunning Universe,
Be A Part Of 'Zodiac' Modern Western Astrology...
Throw 'Twelve' Divisions Of Signs,

Just 'Buzz Me' On When I Might Be Free...
From The Busiest World,
The 'Last Place' You Can Find Me At Home...
Where My Mind Would Be Sleep,

Having 'Network Site' Take Me Off...
On Imo, Whatsapp, Viber And Facebook,
I'm 'Dying To Pick' Traditional Attire...
To 'Gear Up' With Baby Pink Colour,

To 'Order' Pure Chocolate Truffle Pastry;
And Fresh Fruits 'Rejuvenate' Me For A Day,
Have A Newspaper And Watch News Bulletin...
'In The Morning' Get Informative,

Big Screen 'Idol Joins One' Who Achieved;
Their Goal With Unique Quality,
'Resolution For The Future' Is To Be Stand...
On My Own Foot With Positive Aspect,

Just Come Down To The 'Outdoor Activity'...
Is To Play 'Badminton And Kabaddi',
Life 'Excited Me' To Raise India...
With The Flourish Hand Of An Indian People,

One Thing Like To 'Erase From My Past'...
When Ghastly Calamity Dropped;
The 'Little Boy' Atomic Bomb On Hiroshima,
My 'Dream City' Tend To Be More Dreamed;

Where I Do 'Craziest Thing' I've Ever Done,
To Describe Life In Meddling Smash Book;
Is Not A Word Or Two Word Sense;
But To Take Grant For A Best Achiever,

'Wildest Fantasy' Is To Fly...
Onto The Body Of 'Flying Anaconda' With My Dearest One,
Enhance, Few Groovy Thoughts;
Make Me Loyal, Adaptable, Kind And Moreover Generous,

So, Let's Talk About...
The 'Best Pal' On The Earth;
Relate Towards 'An Excellent Books'...
Who 'Furnish' Me More Enlightenment,

To Wrap 'Meddling Smash Book' On The Edge;
Feel So Much Fresh...
To Open And It's Touched...
To Make A Blush On My Face,

FLUCTUATING ANTS

Attend To The World Of Insects Flame;
Everywhere Meet Also Across The Ocean,

Be More Than 'Twelve Thousand Species' Of Minor Insects;
Always Come To The Class Of Insecta,
Have Joined An Empire Of Animalia;
Forever My Family Called As Formicide,

To Carry 'Six Legs' Besides 'Antenna' Over The Head;
So; Fluctuate At Different Phase,
Be 'A Wingless Wings' Of Female Ant;
Wings Ruled 'Queen' And On The Males,

Screeching More And More To Gather;
Survive 'Three Kinds Of Ants' In A Colony,
Be Extended 'Millions Of Babies' Since Centuries;
And Displayed 'Better Team Work' In A Society,

No Worries About 'Amount Or Size' At Any Time;
But 'Shape Do Upset' To 'Giant Mammal' Mind,
'Brown And Black My Colour' But Get Tears At Times;
Because We 'Don't Have Ears' Only Hears While Signs,

We 'Ant Stands On Inspiring Lesson' For All Human;
To Boost Up 'Unity Of Strength' While Marching,
Ate Lot Of 'Sugary Sweets' Then Go Off Frenzy;
We All 'Tiny Ants' Do Work Hard All Times,

Free From 'Any Disorder' To Eat Too Much Sugar;
Thank God! Not 'Any Suspicion' To Make 'An Ally' Of Sweets,
To 'Pack Of Potentialities' Make Things Possible;
Also 'Will Power Strong' To Take Good Decision,

Slowly...Slowly...At A Snail's Pace...
Fluctuating Ants 'Raise Their Tempo' With
Encouraging Songs,
Attend To The World Of Insects Flame;
Everywhere Meet Also Across The Ocean,

WEDDING DOT COM

No 'Rules Follow' Only Surf A Matching Mate...
To Best Combine On Online,
Push 'The Hope' And Carry 'A Heart';
To Take The Grant Of Existing Profile,

As Profile Grows Then 'Another Site' Close Up;
A Curious Tone 'Vibrate' On The Mind,
Just Chill Out To Find 'A Nice Bride And A Nice Groom';
For A 'Whole Life' Of Wedding Bind,

To Touch 'The Sense' Of Perfection;
It Embraces 'All Good Things' For Future Connection,
A Warm Welcome Regards...
As Soon As 'Wedding Bell' Starts 'To Display' On Cards,

To Attend All World Wedding;
There Is No Need To Convey...
The Message To Regards,
Fortunately 'Wedding Calls' To Prepared Mind,

While 'Two People' Acts As An Art Of Sunshine;
Wedding Is Similar Like Branch Of Tree,
Where Fruitful Blessings, Wishes...
And Lots Of 'Splendour Smile' Comes Outside,

To Take The Compliments Of Flourish;
Couple Deliberately 'Undertaking' To This Service,
God 'Fills The Wedding' With Faith And Trust;
Then 'Two Will Enough' To Cherish The Love,

No 'Barriers' Of Religion And Creed;
Gave Surety 'On Stamp' From The Paradise Of Crust,
Marriage Is 'A Wonderful Reward' From Lord's Home;
Also Holds 'On Promise' For Forever,

'No Time And Tenure' To Take An Agreement;
Only 'Two Soul Mate' Have Witness To Tie up,
To Exchange 'The Sharing And Caring' Of Love;
So, 'No Pains No Gains' To Carry A Cherish Life,

When 'Wedding' Get Nearer...
Then Various 'Brand' Comes In Mind;
But A 'Pleasing Smile' At Every Time,
Sparkle 'The Glow Worm Light' On The Wedding Night;

Wish To 'Happy Marriage Life' To Both Unite,
'Aroma Of Happiness' Enlightenment...
On The Wedded Couple;
When They 'Take Oath' Together,

Country Compliments, Way Of Wishes, Blessings...
Running Of Gifts And Presents 'To Walk' The Whole Night,
To Take The Bathe Of 'Fresh Approval' Towards The God;
Both Brace Flourished 'To Seize' The Certificate Of Pleasure,

OH! LOST MY LIFE

Life...What Does Life Stand For? I Asked Myself;
But A 'Spirit Voice' Came To My Flowing Heart,

And Spoke Loudly...Oh! My Dearest Pal;
Life Is Severe...Since A Long Ride...
Have Filled Of Ups And Downs,

Hit And Crash And Undoubtedly;
Achievements And Disappointments Be On Round...
Alike, The Peak Burden Enclose,

To Bear In Life Is Self...
For The Most Hard Thing;
To Deal With Is Self,

Thus, Man Should Be Ready...
To Face Life Eye To Eye;
Nevertheless, How Much I Loved My Time,

And It Has Gone Away...
My Friend, I Know The Worth Of Life;
Having Lost My Life, I Knew That,

Life Without Trust Is A Night Without Day...
Life Without Hope Is A Year Without Spring...
Life Without God Is A Teen Without Parents...

Still You Can Give Without Loving,
But You Can't Love Without Giving...
The Tears Have Dried;
Except The Sorrow Shall Never Die...

WORLD MAP GRILL

Welcome 'Google Earth' You Are...
My 'Virtual Globe' And Created By Keyhole,

Open The 'Keyhole World' Being Alive...
On 'A Single Sheet' To Record In Mind,
To Sit On A Chair 'In an Eastern India' ;
Wave Of My Finger 'To Cross' My Largest City,

Through Walk The Worldly World;
At A Glance In My 'Native Land' With Twinkling Eyes,
Let's Go And 'Explore' A Theory On Geography;
And Find Any City Or Countryside,

By 'Geographical Range' To Tag On India...
Became 'Seventh-Largest Country' In The World,
No Doubt 'Considered' Part Of The South Asia Region...
To Salute "Tricolour",

The Entire Countries, Provinces, States, Territories...
'Scattered' The World Population,
Say A Few Words Of Mouth;
Spread 'An Untold Story' With Full Of World History,

Tie With 'Four Mates' North, East, West And South...
All Meet On Pole Hemisphere,
Drew A Circle 'On Map' In The Solar System;
Earth Shown 'Fifth-Largest' Planet,

How Far Distance Of It...
Be Eight Thousand Miles Diameter,
To See 'Earth Day' On Twenty Second April;
Moves 'Around The Sun' On Its Own Axis,

Though The Shaking Of The Earth's Crust;
Creates The Earthquake,
Take A Ride Of Largest Arabian Peninsula;
'Seventh Continent' Lies On The Fifth Ocean,

Look At The Glaciers...
A Crystal Clear 'White Large Blocks' Of Innovative Ice,
Less Than 'Twenty Five Centimetre' Of Rainfall;
In A Year To Declare 'Desert',

'Barbary States' On Where...
Stubborn Standing Of Atlas Mountains;
Be a Support Of Largest Hot Desert 'Sahara'...
On 'The World' Links To The North Africa,

Let's Turn To The Dry Region...
Where The 'Amazon' Largest River In The World;
And Bound To The South America,
Though, Truly Astounding...

Moreover 'Mysterious Places' Are...
Never Seen 'On Map' While Discover,
So, A Step Forward To The Storyline;
To Find The 'World Map Grill' On 'Google Earth',

AN EVENING IN THE SHED OF MOTHER'S BLESSING

There Is Nothing 'In The Sense Of God' Except Shed Of Love;
Cause Of Eve: His Hand 'Has Blessed' To Produce A Mother...
None Another Than 'One To Took On Womb';
We All World 'Given Named' Blessed Mother Mary,

Heavenly Heaven Creature: Being A God's Figure Foster...
Always Shown 'In The Image' Cast Best 'Onto The Ground',
Mother Is A Natural Close Up Image Of God;
She Is Nothing But 'Miracle Of Almighty Lord',

To Be A Hectic Day: Hone Her Talent With Divine Love;
Then: She Become The 'Super Power Gift' From The Lord,
Be Grateful And Highly Obliged: To Make
A Wonder On Earth;
We All Country's Blessed: To Get 'A Shed Of
Nurture' For Child,

No Hurry In A Way: To Express Of Mother's Love;
Only Gear Up Of Herself: With Account Of Smile,
No Line Of Control 'Of Mother's Blessing';
Cause Burning Blaze Of Mother's Love Always Flawless,

No Comparison: Mother Stands Like Branch Of Tree;
Where She Spreads Her Love As A Leaf,
A Novel Composes A Story At A Time;
But 'Beloved Mother' Makes Numerous Histories In Records,

Mother's Walk Seems To Be An Alarm Clock;
When She Walks Like A Cat Walk...
Always Smile With Morning Clock;
And Jog Her Step Among The Active Day,

God Gave Her A Delightful Degree;
So: Only Speaks On Mother's Simplicity,
She Holds 'Her Personalities' Be Versatile Qualities Of Nature;
There Is Nothing To Hide: But Nearby Judging Quality,

Being A Package Of Stunning Love;
Spread To The Different Artery Of Heart,
Precious Mother You Are 'A Chemist' Of God;
Cause 'Always Make A Treatment' Of Broken Heart;

I Never Be Stressed And All Pain Moved Out And On;
When My Head 'Put Down' In The Shed Of Mother's Love...
She Is Adorable, Delectable And Gorgeous At One Time;
And I Do 'Excellent Job' In The Shed Of Mother's Blessing,

DOUBTFUL THOUGHT

"Ring, Ring... From An Active Brain,
A Cohesive Thought... Link To The Man,
Bulk Of Wise... Comes To The Set Wits Of Mine,
Oh Man! Loop Up With Your Sight;
Where The Mind Clog With Mine,
Have Amazed... To See An Artistic Thought;
Also Growing With Gallop Mind,
Let's Hope To The Superlative Wits...
Besides Any Doubtful Thought;
Yeah! Though Gets An Hopeful...
Gives-An Optimum Feeling,
An Immense Sensation... Coz Of Ruling Mind,
Over The Superb Thought...It Takes A Little Time,
Bravo! A Man With Good Thought;
Takes A Massive Mind,
Have Fun With Dizzy Glory...
To Move Onto Step Further;
A Glittery Wisely In My Memory,
Knowing That...A 'Doubtful Thought' With Anyone Memory",

A CUP OF HAPPINESS

The Prologue Makes Me Sense...
'A Million Dollars Smile'; To Seek Way Of Living Style,
So, Seeing 'A Glad On Your Face';
Grant More Pleasure Than Intake Chocolate,

Famed Saying-'Face Is The Index Of Mind'...
While A Photographer Click Before Taking Snap "Smile Please",
That Is Why: Cheery Face Is Better;
Than A Understanding Heart,

And Well Works Like An Ace;
A Cup Admires To An Individual...
While 'Happiness' Throws The Courage Of Life;
Be Easily Sort Out Issues,

World Recognized Superpower America's State...
Ex President 'Abraham Lincoln' Gave Views On Smile:
"Mostly Spent Alone' But In Garishly Mood;

Usually Rely On 'Comic Books' To Refresh My Mind
With Smiling Face",

God Gifted Us A Kindly, Protectively And Flavour Mother;
Who 'Obliged'...To This Disturbed Universe,
Overly, Joy Works As Work As Mother's Actual Love;
Elsewhere 'A Drop Of Smile Get Down In A Versatile Cup
With No Dead Lines Of It',

To Take A Sip Of Glee...
Barely Gives Sooth By Heart,
Much More Smile Depicts Crocodile Tears Release...
If Truth Be Told: Only One Delight In This Life,
'To Love' And 'Be Loved',

Some Proverb Say: Charity Begins At Home...
And I Say: Smile Begins 'Till A Cup-Full With Happiness',
My Views Tend To See This Universe;
With A 'Positive Way' That Is Happiness,

Do Not Come From Any Shop Or A Supernatural Power...
Or Any Celebrity Or Any Source Of Work;
Also, Get From Inner Sides...
And A Long-Lasting Chain Unless You Make People Happy,
When It Touch To Your Face 'Few Kilogram Weight Gains'
Onto The Face,

New Research Proves: 'Receiving A Smile From Friends Or Nearest One',
Generates 'Much Higher Levels Of Stimulation' To The Brain;
Rather Than Being Given Money Or Having A Cigarette,

Despite The Importance Of A Smile...
Happiness Relatively 'A Full Package' Of Goodwill Life,
Albeit, Pour A Cup With Full Of Smile;
While Your Face Any Setback Coz It Works As Medicine,

AN ORATOR LEAD TO CALENDAR

Catch A Name Of Julian Gregory...
Poured 'An Annual Image' On The Calendar;
Datebook Chap Joins To Every Month...
And Take Off The Trip To Walk Down,

Every Month Stands On Twelfth Comrades...
Who Said Their Month's Teller,
Each Month 'Strive By Design' On Purpose;
While Histories Overlap On Image,

Opening Month To Wish...Happy New Year...
Have Thirty First Day Of Shaking January,
To Pick Twenty Eight Days Yearly: Little
Third Month Of Winter;
Where 'Welsh Calls' February 'Y Mis Bach',

Twenty Ninth Days Recall;
A Leap Year...

Oh! Appears During Four Year;
So: Saxon Termed 'Cake Month',

March 'Be On' Birthday's Mine...
Goes On Crazy 'Baby Mind',
Eight Of March Celebrates...
To 'Women's Day' On The Eve,

First April...
To Cut The Goose,
Flourish Of 'Naive Trade' And 'Japanese Fiscal';
So, Say Goddess Venus Month,

A Sign Of 'Fertility' Occurs A 'Greek Goddess' Maia...
Which 'Named' After 'The Month' Of May,
All The Universe 'Cheers' To 'The May'
In United Kingdom;
Where 'National Smile' Month Celebrates,

June In The 'Summer Month' Of Twenty First...
Or Twenty Second Thrives The 'Longest Day' Of The Year,
To Pause A Game In June; Do Well In Centre Court...
Of 'Worldwide English Tennis Tournament
Wimbledon' Starts New,

To Hit An Hot So Long Day Remains...
Where 'July Calls' The 'Dog Days Of Summer',
Greatest 'Triumph Of Augustus' Occurred This Month;
And 'Renamed' The Month Of Sextilis,

Good Time With The Teachers...
On The Day Of Fifth September;
Dr. Radhakrishnan Grants Celebration To Honour,
Then Entire India Celebrates...

'World Tourism Day' On Twenty Seventh September,
After 'Happiest Day' To Fill 'The Feeling Of Memories'...
On Twenty Ninth September;
Beat Of Every Heart On 'World Heart Day',

October Brings Apple Day...
Celebrated On Twenty First;
So 'Nation' Does Happy Smile...
In The United Kingdom,

World Superpower Country's Hold...
Elections As In The United States;
Be On The Tuesday...
After The First Monday In November,

So; Twenty First Or Twenty Second Day Of Winter...
Of Last Count 'The Shortest' Day And 'Longest Night';
Which Takes 'The December' Bright At All Night,
Come On 'Cookie' Come On 'The Day Of Fourth December'...
Celebrates On 'National Cookie Day',

CELEBRATION OF CELEBRITY

All The 'Red Carpet' Rush;
To 'Blink With' Versatile Crush,
Be Alive To 'Bright Personalities'...
Have 'Calculated' To All Celebrities,

If You Born With A Lay Man;
No One To Take You Lying On,
Celebration 'Whine Pour' With Shine;
A 'New Emo' Web On The Dusky Day,

No 'Cause Of Celebration' To Touch Only;
Greet Of People 'Have Welcome' To Wide Smile,
No Makeup Or No 'Shed Of Fake Light'...
Only 'Happiness' Comes With 'Credit Of Life',

No One Tell 'Only An Agreement' With Smile;
To Display 'On The Floor' Twenty Four Hours 'On Time'...
Hats Of Salute To Gave Naive Proof;
Where Celebrities 'Make Fun' And Meet To Celebrates,

So Many Things 'Hide' Behind To Carry A Fake Smile;
It's All The Time 'On Celebration Line'...
To Meet Of Stardom: Followed By 'Thanksgiving' Greet;
To Get Together 'A Unique' Calendar Day,

A Clear Image 'To Clicked' Of Happiness;
One By One Come Up To...To Take Off Shutter Down,
Patch On 'Remarkable Memory' To Express;
Towards The 'Ceaseless Beauty' Of Eternal Love,

All The Sprinkle Lights 'Cuddling To' The Gladness Time;
To Take 'The Shower' Of 'Attentive Shine',
Beating Of Cheerless, Speechless Moment;
When I Through 'Under The Shed Of'
Celebration Of Celebrity,

Celebration Took Place In Organized Way...
While Evening Was 'Getting Down' With
Inexperienced Desire,
So, 'A Big Applause' To Make A Day Special;
That Stand 'In A Row Of Lively Communication',

Embraced Of Happiness 'With Smile' To Tell A Pride;
Every Moment: 'I Enjoy...Enjoy...And Enjoy',
Alas! Let's Have Presume When A Celebrity Dies;

Then We All World's Go Into The Cheerless,

Celebrity Dies 'At Once' But Their 'Follower Dies' Everyday;

Also Celebration Make Die Hearted...

COMPLIMENTARY COMPLIMENTS

Touchwood! Be Blessed To This Complimentary Earth;
Be Alive Valuable Compliments,
A Journey Of Soul Divided Into A Perfect Goal;
Whereas Plan To An Appreciation Of Joy,

Expressing Of 'Compliments' Be An Ideal Of Trust;
Thus It's Worth More Than Complimentary,
So; Complimentary Seems Like Maize;
While It Splits 'With Popcorn' Then Exhibits Blush,

Compliments Grant 'Genuine Feeling' Of Touch;
Where All 'The Wire Of Soul' Vibrates Till The Mind,
How Individual Catch The Kind Word?
Though 'To Touch With The Thanks'
Of Faultless Compliments,

Whole Depends On The Receptor,
While Priceless Emotions Come Out;
Every Mode On Frequent Action,
Thanks With Regards....Thanks With Regards,

Under The Shed Of Complimentary Compliments;
Humanly Trial Let's Have All The Wipes,
I Have Stunning Mind Where...
All 'The Praises' Arrive In An Approving Way,

Be Beautiful 'Of My Eyes' Till The End Of Life;
All The World Is In My Sight,
My Tongue Is Truly Refined;
And It Taste 'All The Flavour' Off Sweet Bite,

Sometimes 'My Sheet Of Face' Blushes;
Cause All The 'Compliments Expose' On It,
To Be A 'Precious Smile' To Grant;
While Smile Hardly For Good Things In Life,

Never Chat A Lips Alone...
Teeth Support To Jaws On,
When It Touch To High...
And 'Lesser Maw' To Make Sense,

Though: My Ears Have Widen When...
It Takes 'Lot Of' Complimentary Compliments,
Be An Exchange Of Feeling;
It Reflects To The Chain Of Mile,
So; Give 'A Cross Smile' On A While,

My Head Always Bow Down;
Towards The Organizing Creature,
From The Time When...
It Hold Me 'Full On' With Flattering,

DIGITAL WORM

What Does It Mean? It Means A Freak Sound...
Of Common Sense At Present World,
Though, The Whole World Interacts!
With The Globalization By The Same Design Of Interest,

Be An Online Communications...
Or Busiest Schedule To Work Load;
For Twenty Four Hours,
Apparently, Yes...

'Be Tweet' Lying On The System...
With Contact Through Different Modes As On,
On Account Of;
Digital As Works As Like A Stunning Plot...

While Worm Creep Like As Transformation,
Though, To Roast An Immense Procedure...
Of Versatile Features;
Of Mass Media Intake,

We The People Of Universe...
Indulge In Breaking News And Spoil;
The Television World Into To,
For: 'Fighting Fit' Anything New; Anything New...

Have 'Scattered Of Social Media' On 'The News Stuff',
Give A 'Bursting Attention' To An Electronic Media...
Travel To 'All Day And Night' With Rotational Shifts;
By The People Of World Around,

So, Lot Of Questions...
Grow Up From The Breathing Mind;
Who The Creator Of Digital Worm?
Sometimes My Living Intellect Stays;

Me At Hold...
Wait 'For Sometime' My Existing Dear One;
To Reply Your Answers By Another Creator,
Google Say The Idea Of Giving Birth Of Mine;
Grappling The Shared Network Of Connection...
To Worth Other Third Industrial Revolution,

DRAGON ADDICTION

At My Teen Age 'Has Confusing Mind';
Get 'Too Things Quickly' Very Nice,
Make 'To Wish Online' For Something;
Like 'Tough Desire' At Anytime,

Walk 'On Floor' With Fine Craving;
'Hangs On' The Whole Society And Universe...
Though; Washed Away Of Negative Things;
For A Life And' Stick On' The Good One,

My Mind By Born Addicted;
While All Novel Brave Starts...
From The Obsessed View,
To Fix 'On Promise Me'...

Bind All 'Goodwill' To Flourish Heart;
Like Growing Young One,
Chase Of 'Human Race' At Everytime;
Be Fond Of 'Rivalry' No One Winner Behind The Game,

Only One 'Beat' Of Them;
Who 'Contribute' The Variable Game,
So: Life Never Be Changed;
And Walk With Fame,

Be 'An Addiction' Of Survival Things...
'Tiny Ride' To Fetch The Drive,
To Get The Thirst Of Goals;
Addicted To Let's Have A Chance To Try,

So, My Soul 'Addicted To Search' Eerie Place;
Where Usually Set Out To Past Put,
Found 'A Ghoul' Of My Past;
Who Spooked Me At All,

So, Away To Think It Again;
Hey! Steal A Look Of My Dream,
While Dragon Addiction 'Now' Not Here On,
Why You Are? To Be On My Fluctuated Mind;

Cause Of...
'Dragon And Addiction' Since From The Baby Mind,
A 'Chilly Feeling' Had Gone Past;
When I 'Addicted To Have' A Next In My Activist Mind,

Feel Good To Defend My Sight;
Because Every Day I Hold...
Crazy 'Obsessions' Into My Life,
Let's Talk In Evening 'On Refreshments Time';

With My 'Best Pal Of Memory'...
Recalls On Palm,
Constantly, I Wrapped Of Good Habit;
With Closing Of My Life,

Be Survives 'Optimistic One' In An Hollow Life,
So, Soothe My Nerves Calmly...
When My Mumbling Body Bears;
'Desperate' For Desire An Active,

FEARLESS FEARS

It's Been So Long Time...
Without 'My Best Pal' Of Leisure,
To 'Pen Down' To Write Anything;
On The Piece Of Paper,

Count Of 'Fearing Thought's;
Been Already Done,
Lost The Notion Of Wisdom...
Right Now To Bestow Best One,

Then Goes For Fear Something;
On Wrong Thing Forever,
Shudder In My Bone;
To Take 'Default Risk' By Changing The World,

To Know The Peak Grounds;
Inclined Towards 'The Fearless Fear' On And On,
Who Be 'The Next Winner' To Chase The World;
Have Tried For Incredible,

Then, Does Not Mean To Know;
The Reason Of Some Picky Craze,
Become 'A Part' Of The World;
Be Surprised To Lots Of Obstacle Came Here,

Stronger Than Saddened Moreover;
Believer Than Hopeless,
Upon A 'Good Sign' Having A Broken Heart;
Works Like A Symphony,

Fortunately, I Tried For Another One;
Being A Fame For The Proper Link,
Slip 'Your Wish' From The Hand's;
Because 'Life Gives' Only One Beautiful Option,

Behold! The Gone Chance From Binding Palm...
Behold! The Gone Chance From Binding Palm...

Constantly; I Here For The;
Sinless, Fearless 'Miracle Time' Regain,
When Much More Sin Came;
Into My Heart From The Fear,

And 'Realized' Did Innovation To Give...
Magical Thing At All Fussy Time,

'Yeah' Great Innovation Of The Idea;
Being 'A Creative Mind' Of Abstract,

Sometimes 'Be Happy With Fear';
Because 'Always Fear' Goes On Things Positive,
So, When I Think Something Naïve;
Then, 'Fear Brings' A New Hope For Aspirant,

At Ground Level;
I Wish To Have Always...
'Cover Of Shell' With Fearless Fear...
Make 'Things Possible' To Control The Fear,

WET IN THE RAIN

Rain Is An Incoming Feeling...
From The Valve Of Heart,
Pain Is An Outgoing Hope...
From The Corpse Of Sensation,

What A Shared Relation...
To Have Both,
When Rain Get Wet Down...
From The Unlock Sky,

No Stairs, No Technique And No More Cord...
To Come Down,
Only Few Dew Drops On Dry Ground...
Takes Place On The Mud,

Though 'Lots Of Feeling' Stay Alive...
To The Broken Heart,
A Drop Of Tears With Wet Line...
Onto The Face,

Be A Sheet And Telling A Heart Touching Tale,
In The Shed Of Rain...
Each Spirit Recite On Vein,
Alas! Alas! Alas! Alas! Alas!

Be A Touch 'To My Heart'...
Of An English Comic Actor Charlie Chaplin...
"I Always Like Walking In The Rain;
So No One Can See Me Crying",

While One More Teller Depicts...
On The Emily Logan Decens...
"Rain Showers My Spirit;
And Waters My Soul",

Both Have Their Unlike EmotionBut Alike Situation;
Likewise My Consideration Creates Delusive In The Rain,
How It Gives More Pain...
Besides To Get Wet In The Rain,

FRENCH TODDLER TALKERS

Je M' Appelle...Je M' Appelle...Tous A Appelle,
(My Name Is...My Name Is...Has Called All),

Je Suis Indian...Je Suis Indian,
(I Am Indian...I Am Indian),

Quel Est Mon Nom?
(What Is My Name?),

Me Dire Oh! Ma Chère Mère,
(Tell Me Oh! My Dear Mother),

Marcher Sur Mon...Et...Parler Sur Ma Paume;
(Walk On My...And...Talk On My Palm);

Oh! Ma Chère Mere,
(Oh! My Dear Mother),

Bienvenue A La Maison...Quitté Votre Maison...Jouer;
(Welcome Home...Left Your Home...To Play);

Avec Votre Belle Mere,
(With Your Lovely Mother),

Souris Beaucoup...Profiter D'un Lot...Tous Les Jours;
(Smile A Lot...Enjoy A Lot...Everyday);

Je Fais...Maison Sale,
(I Do...Messy Home),

S'amuser...Hangar De Soleil...Nous Rencontrons...A La Fête,
(Have Fun...Shed Of Sun...We Meet...At The Fun),

Commençons...Jouer...Un Jeu,
(Let's Start...To Play...A Game),

Je Compte...Zéro...Un...Deux...Et...Trois,
(I Count...Zero...One...Two...And...Three),

Tous Mes Amis...Préparer Un Jeu,
(All My Friends...Prepare A Play),

Sauter...Et... Vers Le Bas;
(Jumping Up...And...Down);

Et Dis...Avec Unite,
(And Say...With Unite),

Oui...Wow Ohhhh! Lala, Oui...Wow Ohhhh! Lala,
(Oui...Wow Ohhhh! Lala, Oui...Wow Ohhhh! Lala),

Maintenant Tourner...Autre Fun,
(Now To Turn...Another Fun),

De Faire Une Queu...Sur La Piste,
(To Make A Queue...On The Track),

Venir Mon Ami; Bonny Ami,
(Come My Friend ; Bonny Friend),

Etre Dans Une Rangée...De Se Tenir...Un Train,
(Be In A Row...To Stand...A Train),

Oh! Mon Dieu... Oh My Ghosh!
(Oh! My God... Oh My Ghosh!),

Nous Creat...Un Jeu Magique,
(We Create...A Magic Train),

Un Passager Venir...Et...Demande,
(A Passenger Coming...And...Requests),

Excusez-Moi; Cette Place Est-Elle Libre?
(Excuse Me; Is This Seat Free?),

Je Dis...Billet...S'il Vous Plait!
(I Say...Ticket...Please!),

Ami Weldone...Ami Weldone,
(Welcome Friend...Welcome Friend),

J'aime Ça; Oui...S'il Vous Plaît,
(I Like It; Yes...Please),

Donc; Mon Nom...Mis Sur Le Jeu,
(So; My Name...Put On Game),

Oh! Mon Doux...Belle Mere,
(Oh! My Sweet...Lovely Mother),

Nous Avons...Célébrité;...Gagner Le Jeu,
(We Have...Fame;...Win The Game),

Très Bon...Très Bon,
(Very Good...Very Good),

Appeler Mon Nom...Jeu De Bébé,
(Call My Name...Toddler Game),

Nous Sommes; De Notre Mère... Adorable;
(We Are; Our Mother's...Adorable;),

Causeurs...Bébé...Français,
(French...Toddler...Talkers),

MORNING SHINE

'Late Sleep' So Early Woke,
Be 'In A Hurry' Like A Left Life,
'Down The Health' Near The Death;
Oh Dear! What Do You Do?

Why Have Birth On The Globe?
'To Chill The Earth' While Provoke,
Silly! Silly! Silly! Sulky Silly Early Honey;
Like As...Bad Temper Baby,
Baby Peep Out...Smile Out...Teeth Out...
'Look Out' When Sunlight Came Out,

Sunny Shiny Hope 'Binds With Blond Ray';
'Sprinkle' Onto The Baby's Skin,
'Blinking Eyes' Against The Sun;
To Grant 'The Shower' Of 'Vitamin D' By Skin,

'Well Known World' Source Of Sunlight;
So...Body Moves On 'In Action' To Get In Contact,

My Hands Rise 'Incline Towards The Lot Of Flourished;
Be Thanks To 'Dearest Almighty Lord',

Oh Morning Shine! Penetrate To My Mind;
And Break To My Deadline,
To Be To 'Merry And Cheery' On Existence Time;
So: 'Not Flew Joy' On The Way,

Chased Me 'Shine'...Chased Me 'Shine'...
When Life Had Not In My Mind,
To Fix A Game 'Hide N Seek' On Early Shines;
Do 'Check N Mate' From The Beating Board,

Oh Lovely Bloom! Unseen The Sun Light...
'Of Under The Sky' While 'No' Shed Of Shine,
Always Gloom! But 'Plays To Baby's Galloping Mind';
Also 'Create A Seven Colour' Of Sunshine,

'A Ray Of Hope' To Touch Baby's Skin;
On Every Day Like 'A Schedule Of Life Time' Achieve As Do,
Feel Me Delight! Oh Morning Shower;
To Take 'A Ride On Joy' And The Day Blooming Light,

OH GOD!

Shattering Door On The Floor...
Stammering Tongue Boast A Toss,

Lips Sing Lip Be A Tooth;
Whispering Voice Make A Noise,
Puff Away The Glaze On The Face...

Take Off The Veil Behind The Cloak;
Oh God! Who Tap The Door?
Scary Night...Eerie Core!

Beating Heart Be Rolling Corpse;
Something Gone By Well Known,
Oh No...Who Bang The Door?

To Seize The Name Of Idol;
Oops...Dashing Dash Be The Rash,
Gone The Night Made Me Fright...

Take A Stick To Chase Of Clang;
To See The Floor Open The Door,
Oh No...Black Cat Hit The Flap...

Throw The Stick On The Cat;
Meow... Meow! A Screaming Voice,
Then Cat's Came From The Inside...

To Roll The Heart And Be The Mind;
Oh God! Nothing Else In Chilling Night,
No More Than God's Eye...

Be Standing By Surface Side;
I Know Who Mock Me At Dark Night,
Be Nice...Gag Plays My Mind...
Get A Prank Be Always Fine,

OH HELL! CYCLONE CAME

Pushed Back The Past Disaster;
Link 'The Universe' To 'Form A Hole' In Crevasse,
As A Trouble Of The Atmosphere By Tough Wind;
Also Shower Or Snowstorm...

Ostensibly 'A Cruel Steamy Storm';
'Mar Off' The Construction And Make A Rasping Noise,
Cyclone... Originated As A 'Wave Of A Bottomless Untie Split'
Nag In An Awful Temper Manner...

Of Course Not...Unique To Globe;
Merely 'A Portray Of Fat Size' Air Mass,
So As To Rotate In The Order;
Of A 'Sturdy Center' Of Low Atmospheric Pressure...

Innermost Twisting Winds...
Take Turns Oppose;
Anti Clockwise Towards Northern Hemisphere;
And Clockwise In The Southern Hemisphere,

Naming Name Of Cyclones...Hurricanes...Typhoons...
All The Same Through Weather Occurrence,
Different Names Label New Place-Like 'Hurricane';
Terms Incline Onwards Atlantic And Northeast Pacific...

Cyclone Flanked By...
May-June And October-November...
With 'Primary Peak' In November;
And 'Secondary Peak' In May,

Occurs Between Tropic Of Cancer...
Also Capricorn Say Tropical Cyclones,
Alas! World History Recorded...
Thirty Five Deadliest Natural Disaster Stands Into Modern Times,

Get Hold The Name...
Of Two Areas Of Blunder Loss;
Great Bhola Cyclone In Bangladesh...
Had Dated On Twelve November Nineteen Seventy;

Along With Hooghly River Cyclone;
In India And Bangladesh Dated On Seventeen Thirty Seven,
First One 'Troubled Tropical Cyclone' And Struck Then East Pakistan;

Currently 'In Bangladesh' And India's West Bengal,
'Year Turns' Cyclone Name Changed...

Day By Day;
Likes Hudhud, Phyan, Thane, Nilam, Nilofar, Nisha
And So On,
Topsy Turvy Ride Take Glue In Tornado Side,

Wall Of Hell's Image Came To The Mind...
Wash Away The House Of Destroying Sheet;
Borrow Of Confusing Enquire Shore...
Oh Hell! Cyclone Came;

My Lord! Save Our Life...
Otherwise Would Reflect All Earth's Life;
May Be You Giving Fresh Life But...
From The 'Hell Of Fading Breathe' Into Engaging Around,

ONLINE SHOPPING

Enter Into The 'Shopping Site' To Check The Views;
No Baskets, No Trolleys And No Burden 'To Carry' Intense Baggage,

Different Site 'To Seize' The Affordable Price;
And No Compromise 'To Deals' With Low Price,
Surety To Proffer 'On Quality' Towards The Seller Side;
Though Only 'A Particular Deadline' To Meet On Products,

To Set The 'Communication Preferences' At All Sites;
So: Emails Offer 'Booming Discount' On Purchasing Price,
Very Nice...Very Nice On 'Credible' And Hassle Free Site;
All The 'Judging Quality' Based On The Warranty Time,

Customer 'Smiles And Satisfy' To Click The Offer Zone;
After 'Comparing The Seller's Price' To Take An Advice,
'Bags Of Serving Hand' To Grasp The Customer Details;
Get A Hold 'The Festive Fever' By Year On Time,

'Dispatch An Order' And 'Fulfil The Desire' Of Customers;
Bring Up 'The Products' With A Gift Of Smile,
There Is 'No Matter' While Stuff Are Too Late;
Be 'On Registered Name' Quick Delivery On One Complain,

A Variety 'Of Manufactured Goods' Come Under The Shopping Mart;
Enhance 'Shopping List' Stretch To 'A Viral Twist' While Shower Of Discounts,
All Fluctuating Sales 'Open' When Discounts Are High;
So: Limited Offer Apply 'An Online Shopping'
At Alarming Rates,

RIPENESS OF AN OLD AGE

Once Upon A Time At An Age Of Nine;
It's A Flourish 'Heyday' Tale Of Mine,

Filling 'The Idea' Of Dues Memory...
This Is 'The Theme' Of Cruel Ageing Story;
Untold Story Starts With Dropping Leaves,

An Old Age Eyes 'Gaze' Erratic Life With Sight...
To Collect 'The Fruitful Thoughts' Of Teen Age;
An 'Yell Child' Icon Set At The Back Of Soft Mind,

Have 'Learnt' Two Plus Two Is Equal To Four...
Then All Calculation Fade Away;
Become The Age Of Old Stage,

Sterilized To 'Untold Chat' Of Maturity...
And Gazed Innocent Wits;
Then 'My Real Dreams' Had My Wings,

'Until God's Hand' Walk With At Every Time...
Neither 'A Legend' Narration;
Nor 'A Gist' Of Star Plot,

'At The Eleventh Hour' My Twilight Age...
Portrays A Fresh Story;
Be An Idealistic Time,

As Well As 'To Take' A Valiant Step...
The Whole World Add On;
To Reveal My Story,

Had Cranky 'My Mind' To Describe The Feeling...
Of Dynamic 'Child' On That Time;
So, Share 'My Emotions' Time To Time,

Having 'Face To Face' Of Teen Age...
And Ripeness Of An Old Age;
All Of A Sudden Both Age See Eye To Eye,

Out Of Sight...Out Of Mind...My Losing Fault Age...
Shrinks All The Fresh Mind;
And Say It's A Bed Time,

No Say To Manipulate New Story...
Only My Tale Expose;
To World's Best An Odd Days,

Getting 'An Old Person' Indulge Into Brown Study...
Always Played 'A Positive Role' With Playfulness;
By And By 'Sceptic Mind' Lost Of Passion,

When 'Flaky Moments' Flooded By Complains...
It's Not A Cock And Bull Story;
Other Than A 'Dead Silence' Factual Story,

TRUE LOVE

No Matter.. Free From Anxious,
How Far You Are............................ Be A Long Distance Relationship,
Being An Angel...............................Trust You Blindly,
Inside My Heart................................Until Alive,
A Ray Of Hope................................ By God's Blessing,
Is Always In My Pumping Heart....... While Admired You,
Hollow My Mind............................... Nothing Except You,
Be A Senseless Feelings......................Heavenly Warm Touch,
Comes Out Anytime...........................Never Lose You,
I Love U Much More
I Love U Much More,
Be With Love.....................................Have Smiled Mind,
No Wanna Pessimists..........................Think Always Positive,
No Fear Of Being Trapped...................Chose True Love,
You My Honey....................................Be A Delightful,
Coz A Dew Drop.................................Like A Precious Pearl,
On A Sensitive Feeling..........................Be A Kind,
Which Can Be Taken For Heart ....Granted By Spiritual Soul,

And Is A Bonny Feeling At All............Unpredictable Beauty,
If We Leave It Alone................................No Comparisons,
Then It Goes To Insane..............................Of Heartless Feeling,
Oh! My Love...For My Nearest One,
Loved Me Much More
Loved Me Much More
Let It Be A Silent Soul............................Do Not Disturb Of Soul,
Be With A True Love...................................Till True Love Alive,

WELCOME TO KITCHEN SHOW

On Top Of 'The Creature' To Blessed The Chime;
By My 'Frequent Hand' Does Set In Mind,

Topsy Turvy'Ingredients' To Alarm Mixing Mind;
Three Ingredients 'To Form' A Plate Ground-Breaking,
To 'Grant An Attention' Of Love, Patience And Sensible Sense;
To Take The 'Name Of Lord's' The Entire Dish Makes
Astounding,

All Ingredients Said 'Same Words' To Dinning People;
When 'Tummy' Must Extra To Put On Hungry,
While Assemble 'To Welcome' In Lord's Kitchen;
Opening 'All The Items' Get Me Surprised,

Until 'An Exclusive Dish' Ready To Organize For Gathering;
Well 'Party Time' Roll On To Whole Night,
Yahoo! Cooking Style Makes 'The Dish' Delicious;
Where 'Different Items' Cooked Magically On,

Be 'A Garnishing Touch' On Creative Mind;
So, Every Recipe Describe 'Lyrically Stay' Alive,
No Warranty 'To Preserve' All Dish For A Long Time;
But My 'Fanatic Mind' Creates A Box File,

To Display In 'A Piece Of Page' Of Cleaning File;
So 'Wrote An Wonderful Work' To Follow Hygiene Rules,
Get Set Ready 'To Chase' Blessed My Precious Time;
Having Take My Dish 'Get Sentiments' At All Leisure Point,

Smoke In Kitchen 'To Get Me' An Active Moment On Time;
Wait For 'Delightful Dinner' Cause Of No Compromise,
Roast Of An Idea 'To Manipulate' My Juggling Dish;
Never 'Drops Hope' When Notice My Mother's Lesson Join,

BOOM OF PRAYER

Thank You So Much: Oh! Almighty God;
Too Things 'To A Good Deal' In A While,

Heavenly You Created Me...
As A 'Beautiful Being' On Present Earth,
My Soul Always 'Stay Alive' To Have Theist...
Coz No More Heart Believe,

Where All Meal Comes From God's Eye...
You Rule On The Whole Universe,
A Booming Tone 'Of Voice' To Touch My Choice...
Come From The God's Home Town,

Oh Kind! Tie A Lot Of Wish...
To Bow Down 'The Head' In Front Of God's Eye,
Stretch The Hand To Praise Of Blessing...
Let Off My Sin; Let Off My Sin,

Blow The Voice Be Drop The Tears...
Oh My Lord! Just Salt Away My Life,
By The Grace Of You...
Pure My Spirit And Flourish Me Fine View,

No Other Creatures Refine Me Fresh...
Be In This World Guidance By You,
Lots Of Dilemma Share With You...
Coz I Only Feel Secure Shed Under You,

Explosion Of Marking Hand...
Seize Maiden Name! To Raise My Boom,
Always Embrace Of Yearning...
You All Carry Out My Constant Craving,

PARADISE RECRUITMENT

There Are 'Rank Holder' People;
Who 'Queue' In The Recruits,
There Is No Passport, No Visa;
To 'Enter' Into The Paradise,

Only A Basic Condition Apply;
Where Finding 'A Good Soul' Into It,
Vacant 'Post' Position Accomplish;
Where 'Sinless' Group Executes,

'Enrolled' By The Superpowers;
'To Fulfil' The Vacant Seat...
Of Seventh Heaven,
Then; Messenger Of God;

Is Also 'Involved' To Take Recruitment Process,
After That; I Am Waiting For My Turn;
To Upmost High...
In Paradise For Lifetime,

Therefore; Got 'Positioned' To Be Safest Place;
Besides The Fake Earth Off,
'To Breathe With Paradise' Not Only 'A Delightful Place';
But Have A Miraculous Sensation,

No Talent; No Tantrums And No Any Tools;
Only Concern 'A Pure Hearted' Set Of Rules,
Along With 'Good People' To Seize Comfort Zone;
And Heaven's Criteria Fill To Next Seat,

Besides This 'Evil People' Missed Of Comfort Place';
And Took Away In Discomfort Zone,
All The 'Hiring Process' Judged By An Untainted Soul;
Where Permission 'To Be Granted' By The Lord,

God's Love 'Merely' For The Good Human;
And 'Free From' The Offense,
Great Idol Really Feels Awesome;
To Take Care Of Fresh Angel In The Heaven,

Though; Really 'Feel Superior' Cause Heaven...
Is The 'Eternal Home' Of Goodwill Creature,
My Heart Has Touched With So Many Loved;
But 'God's Blessed Me' To Touch With My Soul,

AN EPISTLE TO LORD

My Dearest God! To Be Too Blessed...
To Touch This Heaven Like Earth At All,
Provide Me Pleasure, Pain And All Pull Me Out;
Brought Me Your Great Sight,

You Recharged Me Forever The Life;
Get Ready To Energized Me...
Hold On Cradle,
But Why You Alive A Mind In Human Being!

Who Installed Quickly Rather Than Digital,
My Brain Always Drive...
And Works As A Processor,
So, Be An Active Data Store In An Own Heart,

Loads Of Sentiments And Requirements...
Transmit Towards Your Generous Eye's,
I Open My Heart As A Sheet;
Scripted Lot Of Page Without Stopping My Belief,

Pen-Less Letters Going Fast; While Was Writing...
Through The Views Of Mind Goes On,
Sometimes, Might Be Slip On Blunder Mistakes;
So, No Forgiveness Or No Apologies Of My Sin,

How Your Name On Speakers Again And Again...
Oh My God! Oh My Lord! Oh My Idol! Oh My Holiness!
Oh Delightful God! Listen To Your Baby Voice...
Listen To Your Believer; Listen To Your Fan; Listen To Your Creature,

Otherwise; Present Me Your Skype Figure Or Globe Contact;
So That I Might Be Nonstop Ring By You,
Hopeless Hope...
Scan All The Time,

To Be Sit An Idly: My Vision Monitor You...
While Print Out Solution Come By You,
You Put A Memory Chip Onto My Fortune;
And Connect Me To Beloved Mother As Works As Motherboard,

Having Data Retrieval...
To Give Power Supply,

Through The Warm Touch...
Of My Love One Or Dearest One,

Take A Mouse In Your Hand...
You Whole World Control With Power Play;
And Click To Touchpad To Move On,
Thank God! Saved To All In My Memory Chip,

When Indulging In A Spicy Life Of Mine...
Then You Store In A Sound Cards To Fresh Back Up Memory,
Oh My Lord! Your Network Connection Would Never Fail;
While This World Gone To Be Hell And Hell.......,

www.ingramcontent.com/pod-product-compliance
Lightning Source LLC
LaVergne TN
LVHW091815160826
845684LV00039B/16

* 9 7 9 8 8 9 4 9 8 5 9 0 9 *